BOURBON BADASS™

TRAINING MANUAL

bourbonbadass.com

© 2017 Thievery Spirits, LLC
Fred Ruffenach
All rights reserved.

Photos by Erin Trimble Photography

Become a Bourbon Badass!

As a Bourbon Badass™, you don't need rules.
You don't need someone else to tell you what you
should or shouldn't like when it comes to drinking
bourbon.

Your journey is about diving in head first and
discovering what you like. You're not afraid of trying
something new or of rediscovering something you
didn't like in the past.

Using this training manual, you'll develop your own
taste profile and be able to track your preferences
as they change over time.

Remember, there is no right or wrong way to drink
bourbon, only YOUR way. Always take into account
others' opinions and suggestions, but never forget
you are in charge when it comes to your bourbon
adventure.

Enjoy your ride!

DATE _____

NAME _____

DISTILLERY _____

MASH BILL _____

TYPE _____

AGE _____ **PROOF** _____ **PRICE $** _____

AROMA (What does it smell like?)

○ Fruit _____ ○ Wood _____

○ Nut _____ ○ Grain _____

○ Sweet _____ ○ Spice _____

○ Other _____

TASTE (What does it taste like?)

○ Fruit _____ ○ Wood _____

○ Nut _____ ○ Grain _____

○ Sweet _____ ○ Spice _____

○ Other _____

FINISH (How does it feel going down?)

Subtle Warming ○ ○ ○ ○ ○ ○ ○ ○ Strong Burn

What flavors linger?

○ Spice   ○ Nuts   ○ Tobacco   ○ Mint

○ Citrus   ○ Fruit   ○ Sweet   ○ Medicinal

OVERALL RATING ☆ ☆ ☆ ☆ ☆

Where I was when I tasted it: _____

_____

Who I was with: _____

_____

Why I drank it: *(Recommendation, only option, reputation…)*

_____

Did it live up to expectations? Y / N

Additional info: *(Anything unique, bottle type, distillery/brand history…)*

_____

_____

_____

What I liked: _____

What I didn't like: _____

What it reminds me of: _____

_____

Would I buy it again? Y / N

Is it worth the price? Y / N

Would I give it as a gift? Y / N

Is it hard to find in the store? Y / N

DATE _____

NAME _____

DISTILLERY _____

MASH BILL _____

TYPE _____

AGE _____ **PROOF** _____ **PRICE $** _____

AROMA (What does it smell like?)

○ Fruit _____ ○ Wood _____

○ Nut _____ ○ Grain _____

○ Sweet _____ ○ Spice _____

○ Other _____

TASTE (What does it taste like?)

○ Fruit _____ ○ Wood _____

○ Nut _____ ○ Grain _____

○ Sweet _____ ○ Spice _____

○ Other _____

FINISH (How does it feel going down?)

Subtle Warming ○ ○ ○ ○ ○ ○ ○ ○ Strong Burn

What flavors linger?

○ Spice ○ Nuts ○ Tobacco ○ Mint

○ Citrus ○ Fruit ○ Sweet ○ Medicinal

OVERALL RATING ☆ ☆ ☆ ☆ ☆

Where I was when I tasted it: _____

_____

Who I was with: _____

_____

Why I drank it: *(Recommendation, only option, reputation…)*

_____

Did it live up to expectations? Y / N

Additional info: *(Anything unique, bottle type, distillery/brand history…)*

_____

_____

_____

What I liked: _____

What I didn't like: _____

What it reminds me of: _____

_____

Would I buy it again? Y / N

Is it worth the price? Y / N

Would I give it as a gift? Y / N

Is it hard to find in the store? Y / N

DATE _____

NAME _____

DISTILLERY _____

MASH BILL _____

TYPE _____

AGE _____ **PROOF** _____ **PRICE $** _____

AROMA (What does it smell like?)

○ Fruit _____ ○ Wood _____

○ Nut _____ ○ Grain _____

○ Sweet _____ ○ Spice _____

○ Other _____

TASTE (What does it taste like?)

○ Fruit _____ ○ Wood _____

○ Nut _____ ○ Grain _____

○ Sweet _____ ○ Spice _____

○ Other _____

FINISH (How does it feel going down?)

Subtle Warming ○ ○ ○ ○ ○ ○ ○ ○ Strong Burn

What flavors linger?

○ Spice   ○ Nuts   ○ Tobacco   ○ Mint

○ Citrus   ○ Fruit   ○ Sweet   ○ Medicinal

OVERALL RATING ☆ ☆ ☆ ☆ ☆

Where I was when I tasted it: _____

_____

Who I was with: _____

_____

Why I drank it: *(Recommendation, only option, reputation…)*

_____

Did it live up to expectations? Y / N

Additional info: *(Anything unique, bottle type, distillery/brand history…)*

_____

_____

_____

What I liked: _____

What I didn't like: _____

What it reminds me of: _____

_____

Would I buy it again? Y / N

Is it worth the price? Y / N

Would I give it as a gift? Y / N

Is it hard to find in the store? Y / N

DATE _____

NAME _____

DISTILLERY _____

MASH BILL _____

TYPE _____

AGE _____ **PROOF** _____ **PRICE $** _____

AROMA (What does it smell like?)

○ Fruit _____   ○ Wood _____

○ Nut _____   ○ Grain _____

○ Sweet _____   ○ Spice _____

○ Other _____

TASTE (What does it taste like?)

○ Fruit _____   ○ Wood _____

○ Nut _____   ○ Grain _____

○ Sweet _____   ○ Spice _____

○ Other _____

FINISH (How does it feel going down?)

Subtle Warming   ○ ○ ○ ○ ○ ○ ○ ○   Strong Burn

What flavors linger?

○ Spice   ○ Nuts   ○ Tobacco   ○ Mint

○ Citrus   ○ Fruit   ○ Sweet   ○ Medicinal

OVERALL RATING ☆ ☆ ☆ ☆ ☆

Where I was when I tasted it: _____

_____

Who I was with: _____

_____

Why I drank it: *(Recommendation, only option, reputation...)*

_____

Did it live up to expectations? Y / N

Additional info: *(Anything unique, bottle type, distillery/brand history...)*

_____

_____

_____

What I liked: _____

What I didn't like: _____

What it reminds me of: _____

_____

Would I buy it again? Y / N

Is it worth the price? Y / N

Would I give it as a gift? Y / N

Is it hard to find in the store? Y / N

DATE _____

NAME _____

DISTILLERY _____

MASH BILL _____

TYPE _____

AGE _____ **PROOF** _____ **PRICE $** _____

AROMA (What does it smell like?)

○ Fruit _____   ○ Wood _____

○ Nut _____   ○ Grain _____

○ Sweet _____   ○ Spice _____

○ Other _____

TASTE (What does it taste like?)

○ Fruit _____   ○ Wood _____

○ Nut _____   ○ Grain _____

○ Sweet _____   ○ Spice _____

○ Other _____

FINISH (How does it feel going down?)

Subtle Warming ○ ○ ○ ○ ○ ○ ○ ○ Strong Burn

What flavors linger?

○ Spice   ○ Nuts   ○ Tobacco   ○ Mint

○ Citrus   ○ Fruit   ○ Sweet   ○ Medicinal

OVERALL RATING ☆ ☆ ☆ ☆ ☆

Where I was when I tasted it: _____
_____

Who I was with: _____
_____

Why I drank it: *(Recommendation, only option, reputation...)*
_____

Did it live up to expectations? Y / N

Additional info: *(Anything unique, bottle type, distillery/brand history...)*
_____
_____
_____

What I liked: _____

What I didn't like: _____

What it reminds me of: _____
_____

Would I buy it again? Y / N

Is it worth the price? Y / N

Would I give it as a gift? Y / N

Is it hard to find in the store? Y / N

DATE _____

NAME _____

DISTILLERY _____

MASH BILL _____

TYPE _____

AGE _____ **PROOF** _____ **PRICE $** _____

AROMA (What does it smell like?)

○ Fruit _____ ○ Wood _____

○ Nut _____ ○ Grain _____

○ Sweet _____ ○ Spice _____

○ Other _____

TASTE (What does it taste like?)

○ Fruit _____ ○ Wood _____

○ Nut _____ ○ Grain _____

○ Sweet _____ ○ Spice _____

○ Other _____

FINISH (How does it feel going down?)

Subtle Warming ○ ○ ○ ○ ○ ○ ○ ○ Strong Burn

What flavors linger?

○ Spice   ○ Nuts   ○ Tobacco   ○ Mint

○ Citrus   ○ Fruit   ○ Sweet   ○ Medicinal

OVERALL RATING ☆ ☆ ☆ ☆ ☆

Where I was when I tasted it: _____

_____

Who I was with: _____

_____

Why I drank it: *(Recommendation, only option, reputation....)*

_____

Did it live up to expectations? Y / N

Additional info: *(Anything unique, bottle type, distillery/brand history...)*

_____

_____

_____

What I liked: _____

What I didn't like: _____

What it reminds me of: _____

_____

Would I buy it again? Y / N

Is it worth the price? Y / N

Would I give it as a gift? Y / N

Is it hard to find in the store? Y / N

DATE _____

NAME _____

DISTILLERY _____

MASH BILL _____

TYPE _____

AGE _____ **PROOF** _____ **PRICE $** _____

AROMA (What does it smell like?)

○ Fruit _____ ○ Wood _____

○ Nut _____ ○ Grain _____

○ Sweet _____ ○ Spice _____

○ Other _____

TASTE (What does it taste like?)

○ Fruit _____ ○ Wood _____

○ Nut _____ ○ Grain _____

○ Sweet _____ ○ Spice _____

○ Other _____

FINISH (How does it feel going down?)

Subtle Warming ○ ○ ○ ○ ○ ○ ○ ○ Strong Burn

What flavors linger?

○ Spice ○ Nuts ○ Tobacco ○ Mint

○ Citrus ○ Fruit ○ Sweet ○ Medicinal

OVERALL RATING ☆ ☆ ☆ ☆ ☆

Where I was when I tasted it: _____
_____

Who I was with: _____
_____

Why I drank it: *(Recommendation, only option, reputation…)*
_____

Did it live up to expectations? Y / N

Additional info: *(Anything unique, bottle type, distillery/brand history…)*
_____
_____
_____

What I liked: _____

What I didn't like: _____

What it reminds me of: _____
_____

Would I buy it again? Y / N

Is it worth the price? Y / N

Would I give it as a gift? Y / N

Is it hard to find in the store? Y / N

DATE _____

NAME _____

DISTILLERY _____

MASH BILL _____

TYPE _____

AGE _____ **PROOF** _____ **PRICE $** _____

AROMA (What does it smell like?)

○ Fruit _____ ○ Wood _____

○ Nut _____ ○ Grain _____

○ Sweet _____ ○ Spice _____

○ Other _____

TASTE (What does it taste like?)

○ Fruit _____ ○ Wood _____

○ Nut _____ ○ Grain _____

○ Sweet _____ ○ Spice _____

○ Other _____

FINISH (How does it feel going down?)

Subtle Warming ○ ○ ○ ○ ○ ○ ○ ○ Strong Burn

What flavors linger?

○ Spice ○ Nuts ○ Tobacco ○ Mint

○ Citrus ○ Fruit ○ Sweet ○ Medicinal

OVERALL RATING ☆ ☆ ☆ ☆ ☆

Where I was when I tasted it: _____

_____

Who I was with: _____

_____

Why I drank it: *(Recommendation, only option, reputation…)*

_____

Did it live up to expectations? Y / N

Additional info: *(Anything unique, bottle type, distillery/brand history…)*

_____

_____

_____

What I liked: _____

What I didn't like: _____

What it reminds me of: _____

_____

Would I buy it again? Y / N

Is it worth the price? Y / N

Would I give it as a gift? Y / N

Is it hard to find in the store? Y / N

DATE _____

NAME _____

DISTILLERY _____

MASH BILL _____

TYPE _____

AGE _____ **PROOF** _____ **PRICE $** _____

AROMA (What does it smell like?)

○ Fruit _____ ○ Wood _____
○ Nut _____   ○ Grain _____
○ Sweet _____ ○ Spice _____
○ Other _____

TASTE (What does it taste like?)

○ Fruit _____ ○ Wood _____
○ Nut _____   ○ Grain _____
○ Sweet _____ ○ Spice _____
○ Other _____

FINISH (How does it feel going down?)

Subtle Warming ○ ○ ○ ○ ○ ○ ○ ○ Strong Burn

What flavors linger?

○ Spice   ○ Nuts   ○ Tobacco   ○ Mint
○ Citrus ○ Fruit ○ Sweet   ○ Medicinal

OVERALL RATING ☆ ☆ ☆ ☆ ☆

Where I was when I tasted it: _____

_____

Who I was with: _____

_____

Why I drank it: *(Recommendation, only option, reputation…)*

_____

Did it live up to expectations? Y / N

Additional info: *(Anything unique, bottle type, distillery/brand history…)*

_____

_____

_____

What I liked: _____

What I didn't like: _____

What it reminds me of: _____

_____

Would I buy it again? Y / N

Is it worth the price? Y / N

Would I give it as a gift? Y / N

Is it hard to find in the store? Y / N

DATE _____

NAME _____

DISTILLERY _____

MASH BILL _____

TYPE _____

AGE _____ **PROOF** _____ **PRICE $** _____

AROMA (What does it smell like?)
- ○ Fruit _____
- ○ Nut _____
- ○ Sweet _____
- ○ Other _____
- ○ Wood _____
- ○ Grain _____
- ○ Spice _____

TASTE (What does it taste like?)
- ○ Fruit _____
- ○ Nut _____
- ○ Sweet _____
- ○ Other _____
- ○ Wood _____
- ○ Grain _____
- ○ Spice _____

FINISH (How does it feel going down?)
Subtle Warming ○ ○ ○ ○ ○ ○ ○ ○ Strong Burn

What flavors linger?
- ○ Spice ○ Nuts ○ Tobacco ○ Mint
- ○ Citrus ○ Fruit ○ Sweet ○ Medicinal

OVERALL RATING ☆ ☆ ☆ ☆ ☆

Where I was when I tasted it: _____
_____

Who I was with: _____
_____

Why I drank it: *(Recommendation, only option, reputation...)*
_____

Did it live up to expectations? Y / N

Additional info: *(Anything unique, bottle type, distillery/brand history...)*
_____
_____
_____

What I liked: _____

What I didn't like: _____

What it reminds me of: _____
_____

Would I buy it again? Y / N

Is it worth the price? Y / N

Would I give it as a gift? Y / N

Is it hard to find in the store? Y / N

DATE _____

NAME _____

DISTILLERY _____

MASH BILL _____

TYPE _____

AGE _____ **PROOF** _____ **PRICE $** _____

AROMA (What does it smell like?)

○ Fruit _____ ○ Wood _____

○ Nut _____ ○ Grain _____

○ Sweet _____ ○ Spice _____

○ Other _____

TASTE (What does it taste like?)

○ Fruit _____ ○ Wood _____

○ Nut _____ ○ Grain _____

○ Sweet _____ ○ Spice _____

○ Other _____

FINISH (How does it feel going down?)

Subtle Warming ○ ○ ○ ○ ○ ○ ○ ○ Strong Burn

What flavors linger?

○ Spice ○ Nuts ○ Tobacco ○ Mint

○ Citrus ○ Fruit ○ Sweet ○ Medicinal

OVERALL RATING ☆ ☆ ☆ ☆ ☆

Where I was when I tasted it: _____

_____

Who I was with: _____

_____

Why I drank it: *(Recommendation, only option, reputation...)*

_____

Did it live up to expectations? Y / N

Additional info: *(Anything unique, bottle type, distillery/brand history...)*

_____

_____

_____

What I liked: _____

What I didn't like: _____

What it reminds me of: _____

_____

Would I buy it again? Y / N

Is it worth the price? Y / N

Would I give it as a gift? Y / N

Is it hard to find in the store? Y / N

DATE _____

NAME _____

DISTILLERY _____

MASH BILL _____

TYPE _____

AGE _____ **PROOF** _____ **PRICE $** _____

AROMA (What does it smell like?)

○ Fruit _____ ○ Wood _____

○ Nut _____ ○ Grain _____

○ Sweet _____ ○ Spice _____

○ Other _____

TASTE (What does it taste like?)

○ Fruit _____ ○ Wood _____

○ Nut _____ ○ Grain _____

○ Sweet _____ ○ Spice _____

○ Other _____

FINISH (How does it feel going down?)

Subtle Warming ○ ○ ○ ○ ○ ○ ○ ○ Strong Burn

What flavors linger?

○ Spice ○ Nuts ○ Tobacco ○ Mint
○ Citrus ○ Fruit ○ Sweet ○ Medicinal

OVERALL RATING ☆ ☆ ☆ ☆ ☆

Where I was when I tasted it: _____

_____

Who I was with: _____

_____

Why I drank it: *(Recommendation, only option, reputation…)*

_____

Did it live up to expectations? Y / N

Additional info: *(Anything unique, bottle type, distillery/brand history…)*

_____

_____

_____

What I liked: _____

What I didn't like: _____

What it reminds me of: _____

_____

Would I buy it again? Y / N

Is it worth the price? Y / N

Would I give it as a gift? Y / N

Is it hard to find in the store? Y / N

DATE _____

NAME _____

DISTILLERY _____

MASH BILL _____

TYPE _____

AGE _____ **PROOF** _____ **PRICE $** _____

AROMA (What does it smell like?)

○ Fruit _____ ○ Wood _____

○ Nut _____ ○ Grain _____

○ Sweet _____ ○ Spice _____

○ Other _____

TASTE (What does it taste like?)

○ Fruit _____ ○ Wood _____

○ Nut _____ ○ Grain _____

○ Sweet _____ ○ Spice _____

○ Other _____

FINISH (How does it feel going down?)

Subtle Warming ○ ○ ○ ○ ○ ○ ○ ○ Strong Burn

What flavors linger?

○ Spice ○ Nuts ○ Tobacco ○ Mint

○ Citrus ○ Fruit ○ Sweet ○ Medicinal

OVERALL RATING ☆ ☆ ☆ ☆ ☆

Where I was when I tasted it: _____

_____

Who I was with: _____

_____

Why I drank it: *(Recommendation, only option, reputation....)*

_____

Did it live up to expectations? Y / N

Additional info: *(Anything unique, bottle type, distillery/brand history...)*

_____

_____

_____

What I liked: _____

What I didn't like: _____

What it reminds me of: _____

_____

Would I buy it again? Y / N

Is it worth the price? Y / N

Would I give it as a gift? Y / N

Is it hard to find in the store? Y / N

DATE _____

NAME _____

DISTILLERY _____

MASH BILL _____

TYPE _____

AGE _____ **PROOF** _____ **PRICE $** _____

AROMA (What does it smell like?)

○ Fruit _____ ○ Wood _____

○ Nut _____ ○ Grain _____

○ Sweet _____ ○ Spice _____

○ Other _____

TASTE (What does it taste like?)

○ Fruit _____ ○ Wood _____

○ Nut _____ ○ Grain _____

○ Sweet _____ ○ Spice _____

○ Other _____

FINISH (How does it feel going down?)

Subtle Warming ○ ○ ○ ○ ○ ○ ○ ○ Strong Burn

What flavors linger?

○ Spice ○ Nuts ○ Tobacco ○ Mint

○ Citrus ○ Fruit ○ Sweet ○ Medicinal

OVERALL RATING ☆ ☆ ☆ ☆ ☆

Where I was when I tasted it: _____

_____

Who I was with: _____

_____

Why I drank it: *(Recommendation, only option, reputation...)*

_____

Did it live up to expectations? Y / N

Additional info: *(Anything unique, bottle type, distillery/brand history...)*

_____

_____

_____

What I liked: _____

What I didn't like: _____

What it reminds me of: _____

_____

Would I buy it again? Y / N

Is it worth the price? Y / N

Would I give it as a gift? Y / N

Is it hard to find in the store? Y / N

DATE _____

NAME _____

DISTILLERY _____

MASH BILL _____

TYPE _____

AGE _____ **PROOF** _____ **PRICE $** _____

AROMA (What does it smell like?)
- ○ Fruit _____
- ○ Nut _____
- ○ Sweet _____
- ○ Wood _____
- ○ Grain _____
- ○ Spice _____
- ○ Other _____

TASTE (What does it taste like?)
- ○ Fruit _____
- ○ Nut _____
- ○ Sweet _____
- ○ Wood _____
- ○ Grain _____
- ○ Spice _____
- ○ Other _____

FINISH (How does it feel going down?)
Subtle Warming ○ ○ ○ ○ ○ ○ ○ ○ Strong Burn

What flavors linger?
- ○ Spice
- ○ Nuts
- ○ Tobacco
- ○ Mint
- ○ Citrus
- ○ Fruit
- ○ Sweet
- ○ Medicinal

OVERALL RATING ☆ ☆ ☆ ☆ ☆

Where I was when I tasted it: _____

_____

Who I was with: _____

_____

Why I drank it: *(Recommendation, only option, reputation...)*

_____

Did it live up to expectations? Y / N

Additional info: *(Anything unique, bottle type, distillery/brand history...)*

_____

_____

_____

What I liked: _____

What I didn't like: _____

What it reminds me of: _____

_____

Would I buy it again? Y / N

Is it worth the price? Y / N

Would I give it as a gift? Y / N

Is it hard to find in the store? Y / N

DATE _____

NAME _____

DISTILLERY _____

MASH BILL _____

TYPE _____

AGE _____ **PROOF** _____ **PRICE $** _____

AROMA (What does it smell like?)

○ Fruit _____ ○ Wood _____

○ Nut _____ ○ Grain _____

○ Sweet _____ ○ Spice _____

○ Other _____

TASTE (What does it taste like?)

○ Fruit _____ ○ Wood _____

○ Nut _____ ○ Grain _____

○ Sweet _____ ○ Spice _____

○ Other _____

FINISH (How does it feel going down?)

Subtle Warming ○ ○ ○ ○ ○ ○ ○ ○ Strong Burn

What flavors linger?

○ Spice   ○ Nuts   ○ Tobacco   ○ Mint

○ Citrus   ○ Fruit   ○ Sweet   ○ Medicinal

OVERALL RATING ☆ ☆ ☆ ☆ ☆

Where I was when I tasted it: _____

_____

Who I was with: _____

_____

Why I drank it: *(Recommendation, only option, reputation…)*

_____

Did it live up to expectations? Y / N

Additional info: *(Anything unique, bottle type, distillery/brand history…)*

_____

_____

_____

What I liked: _____

What I didn't like: _____

What it reminds me of: _____

_____

Would I buy it again? Y / N

Is it worth the price? Y / N

Would I give it as a gift? Y / N

Is it hard to find in the store? Y / N

DATE _____

NAME _____

DISTILLERY _____

MASH BILL _____

TYPE _____

AGE _____ **PROOF** _____ **PRICE $** _____

AROMA (What does it smell like?)

○ Fruit _____ ○ Wood _____

○ Nut _____ ○ Grain _____

○ Sweet _____ ○ Spice _____

○ Other _____

TASTE (What does it taste like?)

○ Fruit _____ ○ Wood _____

○ Nut _____ ○ Grain _____

○ Sweet _____ ○ Spice _____

○ Other _____

FINISH (How does it feel going down?)

Subtle Warming ○ ○ ○ ○ ○ ○ ○ ○ Strong Burn

What flavors linger?

○ Spice ○ Nuts ○ Tobacco ○ Mint

○ Citrus ○ Fruit ○ Sweet ○ Medicinal

OVERALL RATING ☆ ☆ ☆ ☆ ☆

Where I was when I tasted it: _____

_____

Who I was with: _____

_____

Why I drank it: *(Recommendation, only option, reputation…)*

_____

Did it live up to expectations? Y / N

Additional info: *(Anything unique, bottle type, distillery/brand history…)*

_____

_____

_____

What I liked: _____

What I didn't like: _____

What it reminds me of: _____

_____

Would I buy it again? Y / N

Is it worth the price? Y / N

Would I give it as a gift? Y / N

Is it hard to find in the store? Y / N

DATE _____

NAME _____

DISTILLERY _____

MASH BILL _____

TYPE _____

AGE _____ **PROOF** _____ **PRICE $** _____

AROMA (What does it smell like?)

○ Fruit _____ ○ Wood _____

○ Nut _____ ○ Grain _____

○ Sweet _____ ○ Spice _____

○ Other _____

TASTE (What does it taste like?)

○ Fruit _____ ○ Wood _____

○ Nut _____ ○ Grain _____

○ Sweet _____ ○ Spice _____

○ Other _____

FINISH (How does it feel going down?)

Subtle Warming ○ ○ ○ ○ ○ ○ ○ ○ Strong Burn

What flavors linger?

○ Spice ○ Nuts ○ Tobacco ○ Mint

○ Citrus ○ Fruit ○ Sweet ○ Medicinal

OVERALL RATING ☆ ☆ ☆ ☆ ☆

Where I was when I tasted it: _____

_____

Who I was with: _____

_____

Why I drank it: *(Recommendation, only option, reputation…)*

_____

Did it live up to expectations? Y / N

Additional info: *(Anything unique, bottle type, distillery/brand history…)*

_____

_____

_____

What I liked: _____

What I didn't like: _____

What it reminds me of: _____

_____

Would I buy it again? Y / N

Is it worth the price? Y / N

Would I give it as a gift? Y / N

Is it hard to find in the store? Y / N

DATE _____

NAME _____

DISTILLERY _____

MASH BILL _____

TYPE _____

AGE _____ **PROOF** _____ **PRICE $** _____

AROMA (What does it smell like?)

○ Fruit _____ ○ Wood _____

○ Nut _____ ○ Grain _____

○ Sweet _____ ○ Spice _____

○ Other _____

TASTE (What does it taste like?)

○ Fruit _____ ○ Wood _____

○ Nut _____ ○ Grain _____

○ Sweet _____ ○ Spice _____

○ Other _____

FINISH (How does it feel going down?)

Subtle Warming ○ ○ ○ ○ ○ ○ ○ ○ Strong Burn

What flavors linger?

○ Spice ○ Nuts ○ Tobacco ○ Mint

○ Citrus ○ Fruit ○ Sweet ○ Medicinal

OVERALL RATING ☆ ☆ ☆ ☆ ☆

Where I was when I tasted it: _____

_____

Who I was with: _____

_____

Why I drank it: *(Recommendation, only option, reputation...)*

_____

Did it live up to expectations? Y / N

Additional info: *(Anything unique, bottle type, distillery/brand history...)*

_____

_____

_____

What I liked: _____

What I didn't like: _____

What it reminds me of: _____

_____

Would I buy it again? Y / N

Is it worth the price? Y / N

Would I give it as a gift? Y / N

Is it hard to find in the store? Y / N

DATE _____

NAME _____

DISTILLERY _____

MASH BILL _____

TYPE _____

AGE _____ **PROOF** _____ **PRICE $** _____

AROMA (What does it smell like?)

○ Fruit _____ ○ Wood _____

○ Nut _____ ○ Grain _____

○ Sweet _____ ○ Spice _____

○ Other _____

TASTE (What does it taste like?)

○ Fruit _____ ○ Wood _____

○ Nut _____ ○ Grain _____

○ Sweet _____ ○ Spice _____

○ Other _____

FINISH (How does it feel going down?)

Subtle Warming ○ ○ ○ ○ ○ ○ ○ ○ Strong Burn

What flavors linger?

○ Spice   ○ Nuts   ○ Tobacco   ○ Mint

○ Citrus ○ Fruit ○ Sweet   ○ Medicinal

OVERALL RATING ☆ ☆ ☆ ☆ ☆

Where I was when I tasted it: _____

_____

Who I was with: _____

_____

Why I drank it: *(Recommendation, only option, reputation...)*

_____

Did it live up to expectations? Y / N

Additional info: *(Anything unique, bottle type, distillery/brand history...)*

_____

_____

_____

What I liked: _____

What I didn't like: _____

What it reminds me of: _____

_____

Would I buy it again? Y / N

Is it worth the price? Y / N

Would I give it as a gift? Y / N

Is it hard to find in the store? Y / N

DATE _____

NAME _____

DISTILLERY _____

MASH BILL _____

TYPE _____

AGE _____ **PROOF** _____ **PRICE $** _____

AROMA (What does it smell like?)

○ Fruit _____   ○ Wood _____

○ Nut _____   ○ Grain _____

○ Sweet _____   ○ Spice _____

○ Other _____

TASTE (What does it taste like?)

○ Fruit _____   ○ Wood _____

○ Nut _____   ○ Grain _____

○ Sweet _____   ○ Spice _____

○ Other _____

FINISH (How does it feel going down?)

Subtle Warming ○ ○ ○ ○ ○ ○ ○ ○ Strong Burn

What flavors linger?

○ Spice   ○ Nuts   ○ Tobacco   ○ Mint

○ Citrus   ○ Fruit   ○ Sweet   ○ Medicinal

OVERALL RATING ☆ ☆ ☆ ☆ ☆

Where I was when I tasted it: _____

_____

Who I was with: _____

_____

Why I drank it: *(Recommendation, only option, reputation…)*

_____

Did it live up to expectations? Y / N

Additional info: *(Anything unique, bottle type, distillery/brand history…)*

_____

_____

_____

What I liked: _____

What I didn't like: _____

What it reminds me of: _____

_____

Would I buy it again? Y / N

Is it worth the price? Y / N

Would I give it as a gift? Y / N

Is it hard to find in the store? Y / N

DATE _____

NAME _____

DISTILLERY _____

MASH BILL _____

TYPE _____

AGE _____ **PROOF** _____ **PRICE $** _____

AROMA (What does it smell like?)

○ Fruit _____ ○ Wood _____

○ Nut _____ ○ Grain _____

○ Sweet _____ ○ Spice _____

○ Other _____

TASTE (What does it taste like?)

○ Fruit _____ ○ Wood _____

○ Nut _____ ○ Grain _____

○ Sweet _____ ○ Spice _____

○ Other _____

FINISH (How does it feel going down?)

Subtle Warming ○ ○ ○ ○ ○ ○ ○ ○ Strong Burn

What flavors linger?

○ Spice ○ Nuts ○ Tobacco ○ Mint

○ Citrus ○ Fruit ○ Sweet ○ Medicinal

OVERALL RATING ☆ ☆ ☆ ☆ ☆

Where I was when I tasted it: _____

_____

Who I was with: _____

_____

Why I drank it: *(Recommendation, only option, reputation…)*

_____

Did it live up to expectations? Y / N

Additional info: *(Anything unique, bottle type, distillery/brand history…)*

_____

_____

_____

What I liked: _____

What I didn't like: _____

What it reminds me of: _____

_____

Would I buy it again? Y / N

Is it worth the price? Y / N

Would I give it as a gift? Y / N

Is it hard to find in the store? Y / N

DATE _____

NAME _____

DISTILLERY _____

MASH BILL _____

TYPE _____

AGE _____ **PROOF** _____ **PRICE $** _____

AROMA (What does it smell like?)

○ Fruit _____ ○ Wood _____

○ Nut _____ ○ Grain _____

○ Sweet _____ ○ Spice _____

○ Other _____

TASTE (What does it taste like?)

○ Fruit _____ ○ Wood _____

○ Nut _____ ○ Grain _____

○ Sweet _____ ○ Spice _____

○ Other _____

FINISH (How does it feel going down?)

Subtle Warming ○ ○ ○ ○ ○ ○ ○ ○ Strong Burn

What flavors linger?

○ Spice   ○ Nuts   ○ Tobacco   ○ Mint

○ Citrus   ○ Fruit   ○ Sweet   ○ Medicinal

OVERALL RATING ☆ ☆ ☆ ☆ ☆

Where I was when I tasted it: _____

_____

Who I was with: _____

_____

Why I drank it: *(Recommendation, only option, reputation…)*

_____

Did it live up to expectations? Y / N

Additional info: *(Anything unique, bottle type, distillery/brand history…)*

_____

_____

_____

What I liked: _____

What I didn't like: _____

What it reminds me of: _____

_____

Would I buy it again? Y / N

Is it worth the price? Y / N

Would I give it as a gift? Y / N

Is it hard to find in the store? Y / N

DATE _____

NAME _____

DISTILLERY _____

MASH BILL _____

TYPE _____

AGE _____ **PROOF** _____ **PRICE $** _____

AROMA (What does it smell like?)

○ Fruit _____   ○ Wood _____

○ Nut _____   ○ Grain _____

○ Sweet _____   ○ Spice _____

○ Other _____

TASTE (What does it taste like?)

○ Fruit _____   ○ Wood _____

○ Nut _____   ○ Grain _____

○ Sweet _____   ○ Spice _____

○ Other _____

FINISH (How does it feel going down?)

Subtle Warming ○ ○ ○ ○ ○ ○ ○ ○ Strong Burn

What flavors linger?

○ Spice ○ Nuts ○ Tobacco ○ Mint

○ Citrus ○ Fruit ○ Sweet ○ Medicinal

OVERALL RATING ☆ ☆ ☆ ☆ ☆

Where I was when I tasted it: _____

_____

Who I was with: _____

_____

Why I drank it: *(Recommendation, only option, reputation...)*

_____

Did it live up to expectations? Y / N

Additional info: *(Anything unique, bottle type, distillery/brand history...)*

_____

_____

_____

What I liked: _____

What I didn't like: _____

What it reminds me of: _____

_____

Would I buy it again? Y / N

Is it worth the price? Y / N

Would I give it as a gift? Y / N

Is it hard to find in the store? Y / N

DATE _____

NAME _____

DISTILLERY _____

MASH BILL _____

TYPE _____

AGE _____ **PROOF** _____ **PRICE $** _____

AROMA (What does it smell like?)

○ Fruit _____ ○ Wood _____

○ Nut _____ ○ Grain _____

○ Sweet _____ ○ Spice _____

○ Other _____

TASTE (What does it taste like?)

○ Fruit _____ ○ Wood _____

○ Nut _____ ○ Grain _____

○ Sweet _____ ○ Spice _____

○ Other _____

FINISH (How does it feel going down?)

Subtle Warming ○ ○ ○ ○ ○ ○ ○ ○ Strong Burn

What flavors linger?

○ Spice   ○ Nuts   ○ Tobacco   ○ Mint

○ Citrus ○ Fruit ○ Sweet   ○ Medicinal

OVERALL RATING ☆ ☆ ☆ ☆ ☆

Where I was when I tasted it: _____

_____

Who I was with: _____

_____

Why I drank it: *(Recommendation, only option, reputation...)*

_____

Did it live up to expectations? Y / N

Additional info: *(Anything unique, bottle type, distillery/brand history...)*

_____

_____

_____

What I liked: _____

What I didn't like: _____

What it reminds me of: _____

_____

Would I buy it again? Y / N

Is it worth the price? Y / N

Would I give it as a gift? Y / N

Is it hard to find in the store? Y / N

DATE _____

NAME _____

DISTILLERY _____

MASH BILL _____

TYPE _____

AGE _____ **PROOF** _____ **PRICE $** _____

AROMA (What does it smell like?)

○ Fruit _____ ○ Wood _____

○ Nut _____ ○ Grain _____

○ Sweet _____ ○ Spice _____

○ Other _____

TASTE (What does it taste like?)

○ Fruit _____ ○ Wood _____

○ Nut _____ ○ Grain _____

○ Sweet _____ ○ Spice _____

○ Other _____

FINISH (How does it feel going down?)

Subtle Warming ○ ○ ○ ○ ○ ○ ○ ○ Strong Burn

What flavors linger?

○ Spice ○ Nuts ○ Tobacco ○ Mint

○ Citrus ○ Fruit ○ Sweet ○ Medicinal

OVERALL RATING ☆ ☆ ☆ ☆ ☆

Where I was when I tasted it: _____

_____

Who I was with: _____

_____

Why I drank it: *(Recommendation, only option, reputation…)*

_____

Did it live up to expectations? Y / N

Additional info: *(Anything unique, bottle type, distillery/brand history…)*

_____

_____

_____

What I liked: _____

What I didn't like: _____

What it reminds me of: _____

_____

Would I buy it again? Y / N

Is it worth the price? Y / N

Would I give it as a gift? Y / N

Is it hard to find in the store? Y / N

DATE _____

NAME _____

DISTILLERY _____

MASH BILL _____

TYPE _____

AGE _____ **PROOF** _____ **PRICE $** _____

AROMA (What does it smell like?)

○ Fruit _____ ○ Wood _____

○ Nut _____ ○ Grain _____

○ Sweet _____ ○ Spice _____

○ Other _____

TASTE (What does it taste like?)

○ Fruit _____ ○ Wood _____

○ Nut _____ ○ Grain _____

○ Sweet _____ ○ Spice _____

○ Other _____

FINISH (How does it feel going down?)

Subtle Warming ○ ○ ○ ○ ○ ○ ○ ○ Strong Burn

What flavors linger?

○ Spice ○ Nuts ○ Tobacco ○ Mint

○ Citrus ○ Fruit ○ Sweet ○ Medicinal

OVERALL RATING ☆ ☆ ☆ ☆ ☆

Where I was when I tasted it: _____
_____

Who I was with: _____
_____

Why I drank it: *(Recommendation, only option, reputation...)*
_____

Did it live up to expectations? Y / N

Additional info: *(Anything unique, bottle type, distillery/brand history...)*
_____
_____
_____

What I liked: _____

What I didn't like: _____

What it reminds me of: _____
_____

Would I buy it again? Y / N

Is it worth the price? Y / N

Would I give it as a gift? Y / N

Is it hard to find in the store? Y / N

DATE _____

NAME _____

DISTILLERY _____

MASH BILL _____

TYPE _____

AGE _____ **PROOF** _____ **PRICE $** _____

AROMA (What does it smell like?)

○ Fruit _____ ○ Wood _____

○ Nut _____ ○ Grain _____

○ Sweet _____ ○ Spice _____

○ Other _____

TASTE (What does it taste like?)

○ Fruit _____ ○ Wood _____

○ Nut _____ ○ Grain _____

○ Sweet _____ ○ Spice _____

○ Other _____

FINISH (How does it feel going down?)

Subtle Warming ○ ○ ○ ○ ○ ○ ○ ○ Strong Burn

What flavors linger?

○ Spice ○ Nuts ○ Tobacco ○ Mint

○ Citrus ○ Fruit ○ Sweet ○ Medicinal

OVERALL RATING ☆ ☆ ☆ ☆ ☆

Where I was when I tasted it: _____

_____

Who I was with: _____

_____

Why I drank it: *(Recommendation, only option, reputation…)*

_____

Did it live up to expectations? Y / N

Additional info: *(Anything unique, bottle type, distillery/brand history…)*

_____

_____

_____

What I liked: _____

What I didn't like: _____

What it reminds me of: _____

_____

Would I buy it again? Y / N

Is it worth the price? Y / N

Would I give it as a gift? Y / N

Is it hard to find in the store? Y / N

DATE _____

NAME _____

DISTILLERY _____

MASH BILL _____

TYPE _____

AGE _____ **PROOF** _____ **PRICE $** _____

AROMA (What does it smell like?)

○ Fruit _____ ○ Wood _____

○ Nut _____ ○ Grain _____

○ Sweet _____ ○ Spice _____

○ Other _____

TASTE (What does it taste like?)

○ Fruit _____ ○ Wood _____

○ Nut _____ ○ Grain _____

○ Sweet _____ ○ Spice _____

○ Other _____

FINISH (How does it feel going down?)

Subtle Warming ○ ○ ○ ○ ○ ○ ○ ○ Strong Burn

What flavors linger?

○ Spice   ○ Nuts   ○ Tobacco   ○ Mint

○ Citrus   ○ Fruit   ○ Sweet   ○ Medicinal

OVERALL RATING ☆ ☆ ☆ ☆ ☆

Where I was when I tasted it: _____

_____

Who I was with: _____

_____

Why I drank it: *(Recommendation, only option, reputation…)*

_____

Did it live up to expectations? Y / N

Additional info: *(Anything unique, bottle type, distillery/brand history…)*

_____

_____

_____

What I liked: _____

What I didn't like: _____

What it reminds me of: _____

_____

Would I buy it again? Y / N

Is it worth the price? Y / N

Would I give it as a gift? Y / N

Is it hard to find in the store? Y / N

DATE _____

NAME _____

DISTILLERY _____

MASH BILL _____

TYPE _____

AGE _____ **PROOF** _____ **PRICE $** _____

AROMA (What does it smell like?)

○ Fruit _____ ○ Wood _____

○ Nut _____ ○ Grain _____

○ Sweet _____ ○ Spice _____

○ Other _____

TASTE (What does it taste like?)

○ Fruit _____ ○ Wood _____

○ Nut _____ ○ Grain _____

○ Sweet _____ ○ Spice _____

○ Other _____

FINISH (How does it feel going down?)

Subtle Warming ○ ○ ○ ○ ○ ○ ○ ○ Strong Burn

What flavors linger?

○ Spice ○ Nuts ○ Tobacco ○ Mint

○ Citrus ○ Fruit ○ Sweet ○ Medicinal

OVERALL RATING ☆ ☆ ☆ ☆ ☆

Where I was when I tasted it: _____

_____

Who I was with: _____

_____

Why I drank it: *(Recommendation, only option, reputation…)*

_____

Did it live up to expectations? Y / N

Additional info: *(Anything unique, bottle type, distillery/brand history…)*

_____

_____

_____

What I liked: _____

What I didn't like: _____

What it reminds me of: _____

_____

Would I buy it again? Y / N

Is it worth the price? Y / N

Would I give it as a gift? Y / N

Is it hard to find in the store? Y / N

What Makes Bourbon Bourbon?

Made in the United States

* 51% corn
* Distilled to no higher than 160 proof
* Put into barrel at no higher than 125 proof
* Aged in a new charred oak container
* No added colors or flavorings

Bottled in Bond

* Follows the 1897 Bottled in Bond Act, which created standards for distilled spirits
* Must be aged in a federally funded bonded warehouse
* Made in one distillery, in one season, by one distiller
* Aged at least 4 years
* 100 proof
* Nothing but water can be added

Kentucky Bourbon

* Produced and aged for a minimum of one year in Kentucky

Straight Bourbon

* Aged for a minimum of 2 years; anything less than 4 years requires an age statement

Kentucky Straight Bourbon

* Produced and aged for a minimum of 2 years in the state of Kentucky

Common Terms

ABV / Proof – % of alcohol by volume; in the US, proof is 2 times the ABV

Angel's Share – evaporation during aging

Barrel Strength – indicates no water was added during bottling; it is the same proof as it was in the barrel

Charring – burning the inside of a barrel

Cooperage – where barrels are made

Distillate – the product obtained from the condensation of vapors in distillation

Entry Proof – the proof when distillate is added to a barrel for aging

High Rye – in general, mash bill has 20% rye or higher

Mash Bill – the mix of grains used to make bourbon; typically 3 grains are in every mash bill: corn, rye or wheat, and malted barley

Rickhouse – the building where bourbon barrels are stored

Single Barrel – all bourbon in a bottle comes from a single barrel of bourbon

Small Batch – no legal definition; mingling select barrels to achieve a desired flavor profile

Wheated Bourbon – wheat is the secondary grain in the mash bill

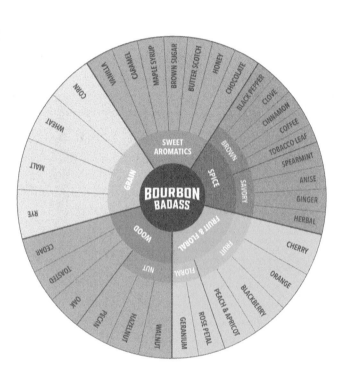

My Favorites

My Favorites